Good Manners

at Play, Home, and School

by Carrie Finn   illustrated by Chris Lensch

PICTURE WINDOW BOOKS
Minneapolis, Minnesota

Special thanks to our advisers for their expertise:

Kay Augustine, Associate Director
Institute for Character Development at Drake University

Susan Kesselring, M.A., Literacy Educator
Rosemount–Apple Valley–Eagan (Minnesota) School District

Editor: Nick Healy
Designer: Tracy Davies
Page Production: Melissa Kes
Art Director: Nathan Gassman
Associate Managing Editor: Christianne Jones
The illustrations in this book were created digitally.

Picture Window Books
151 Good Counsel Drive
P.O. Box 669
Mankato, MN 56002-0669
877-845-8392
www.picturewindowbooks.com

Printed in Malaysia.

Library of Congress Cataloging-in-Publication Data
Finn, Carrie.
Good manners : at play, home, and school / by Carrie
Finn ; illustrated by Chris Lensch.
p. cm. — (Way to be! manners)
ISBN-13: 978-1-4048-5093-4 (paperback)
1. Etiquette for children and teenagers. I. Lensch, Chris.
II. Title.
BJ1857.C5F46 2008
395.1'22—dc22   2008028325

Table of Contents

Manners at the Table

Good manners make mealtime a happy time for everyone. In a restaurant, you can use good manners to show respect for the cook, your server, and other customers. At home, your manners show respect for your family members.

There are lots of ways to use good manners at the table.

Lucy washes her hands with soap before she comes to the table.

She is using good manners.

Peter puts his napkin in his lap. He sits still and stays in his chair during the meal.

He is using good manners.

Ron keeps his mouth closed
while he chews his food.

**He is using
good manners.**

Billy says "Please" when he asks Becca to pass the butter. He says "Thank you" when she does.

He is using
good manners.

Daniel is not sure he will like today's lunch. Still, he tastes everything on his plate.

14

He is using good manners.

Teddy uses his napkin to wipe his mouth. He never wipes his mouth on his shirt.

He is using good manners.

Sarah and Isaac ask to be excused from the table at the end of the meal.

They are using good manners.

Try using your good manners whenever you sit down to eat. Good manners allow everyone to relax and enjoy the meal.

Manners on the Telephone

Using the telephone to call friends or family can be fun. Phone calls can also be very useful in everyday life. Everyone wants to talk without any problems. Good manners on the phone help make that happen.

There are lots of ways you can use good telephone manners.

When he answers the phone, Kyle says, "Hello, this is the Jackson residence."

He is using good manners.

Naomi speaks in a clear voice on the phone. She does not yell or whisper.

She is using good manners.

Lydia answers the phone, but the call is for her brother. She says, "Just a minute, please. I'll get David for you."

She is using good manners.

Bryce says, "Sorry, my mom can't come to the phone right now." He does not tell the caller that his mom is in the bathtub.

He is using good manners.

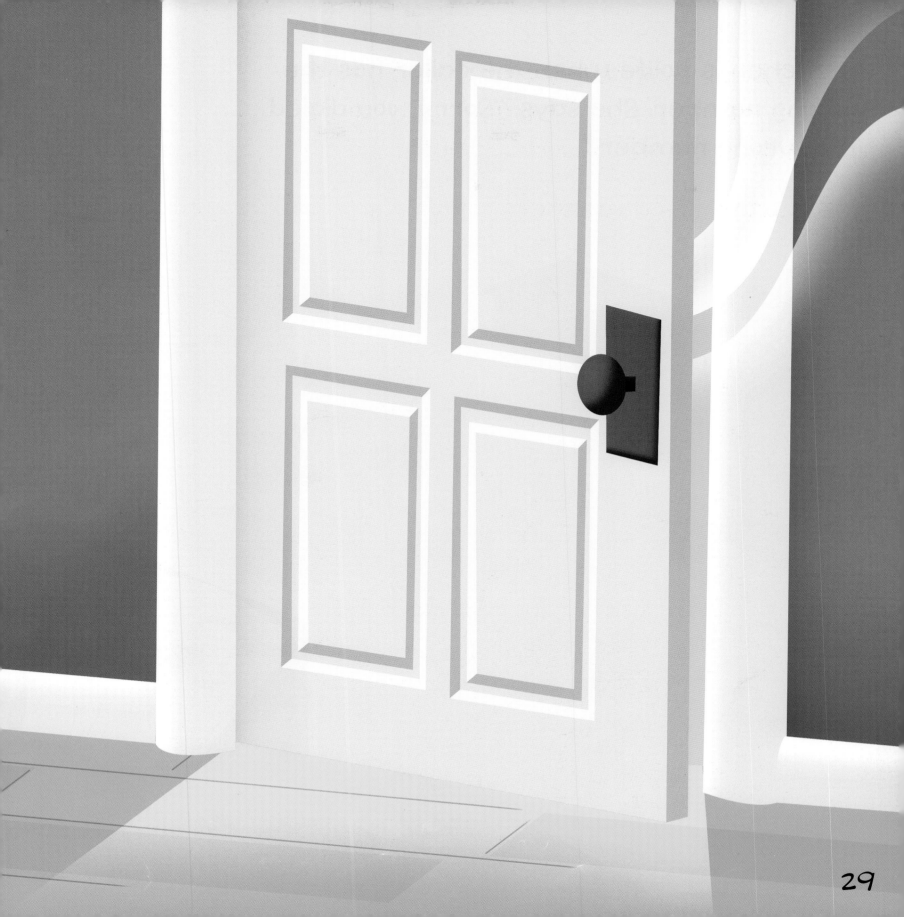

Gretchen is polite when the caller has the wrong number. She says, "Sorry, you dialed the wrong number."

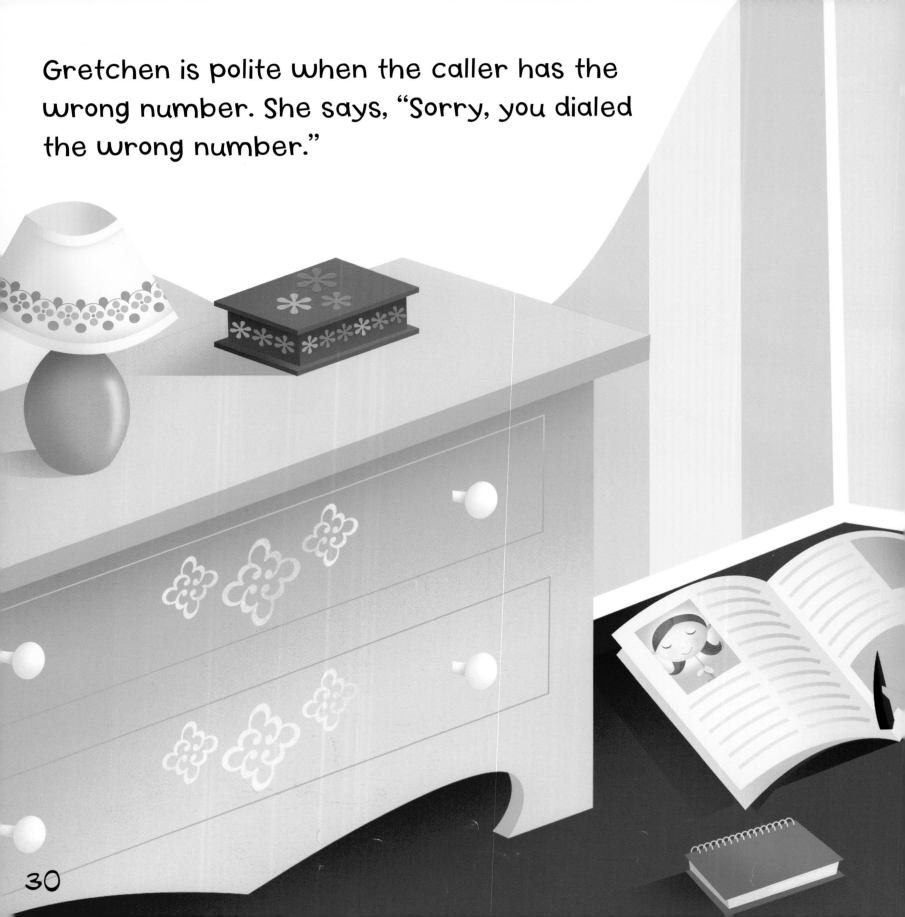

She is using good manners.

Colby needs to talk to Justin, but Justin's mom answers the call. Colby says, "Hello, this is Colby. May I please speak with Justin?"

He is using good manners.

Joanna says "Goodbye and thanks for calling" before hanging up the phone.

She is using good manners.

The telephone is an important tool for many people. Good manners can make the telephone work for you. You can talk to friends and family, and you can be sure you will be heard.

Manners in Public

Whether you are at the park, the movies, or the store, you can use good manners. In fact, good manners come in handy anytime you are out and about.

There are lots of ways you can use good manners in public.

Calvin says "Good morning, Mr. Jeffers!" when he gets on the school bus.

He says "Have a good night, Mr. Jeffers. Thank you!" when he gets off the bus at the end of the day.

He is using good manners.

Erik goes to the pet store to look at fish. He says "Excuse me" when he bumps into someone.

He is using good manners.

Jude uses the sidewalk on his way home from school. He stays out of people's yards.

He is using good manners.

Clara and Mitchell throw their trash in the bin after their picnic in the park.

They are using good manners.

Annika says "Thank you" when the waiter brings her hamburger.

She is using good manners.

Jack loves space movies. Still, he goes to the back of the ticket line at the theater. He waits his turn.

He is using good manners.

Lorna does not shout when she spots her friend Chloe at the museum. She walks over to Chloe and says hello.

She is using good manners.

It's easy to use good manners in your neighborhood, at the store, or in a restaurant. When you do, you will find that people treat you kindly in return.

Manners at School

Your school is a busy place. Using good manners can make it nicer for everyone. Good manners can also help everyone learn. Good manners show respect for teachers and classmates.

There are lots of ways you can use good manners at school.

Olivia gets to class on time each day. She always says, "Good morning, Miss Martin."

She is using good manners.

Arnold gives his full attention to his teacher's directions.

He is using good manners.

seed

water

light

Paul keeps his eyes on his own work. He never peeks at his neighbor's paper.

He is using good manners.

Alan and Cory stand in line quietly before recess.

They are using good manners.

Jamie cleans up her table after art class.

She is using good manners.

Owen raises his hand to ask his teacher a question.

He is using good manners.

It's important to use good manners whenever you are in class. Good manners keep the classroom running smoothly.

Manners on the Playground

The playground is for everyone.

It is a place where people go to have fun. Good manners allow everyone to have a turn. They also help people play safely.

There are lots of ways you can use good manners on the playground.

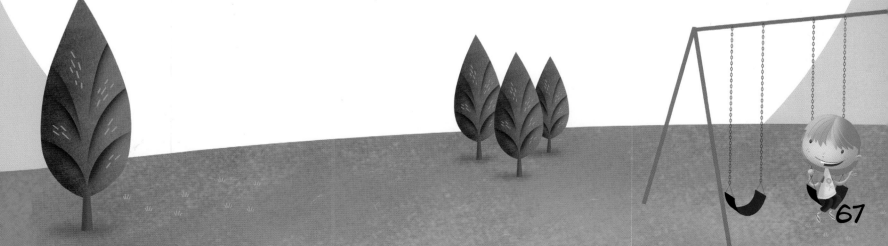

Elliot waits his turn to ride the swing.

He is using good manners.

69

Jacob and Tim listen while the teacher explains the rules of tetherball.

They are using good manners.

Cody says "Good game!" to players on the other team after they win the kickball game.

He is using good manners.

Juan says "Please"
when he asks to use
Kelly's jump rope.

**He is using
good manners.**

Kim helps Jenny get up after she falls down during the soccer game.

She is using good manners.

After recess, Cheryl and Riley pick up soccer balls, baseballs, a bat, and other toys.

They are using good manners.

It's important to have fun and to use good manners when you visit the playground. By using good manners, everyone will get a turn, and everyone can play safely.

Manners in the Library

Good manners are an important part of any library visit. Lots of different people use the library in lots of different ways. By using good manners, you can show respect for everyone.

There are many ways you can use good manners in the library.

Mia uses her inside voice in the library. She keeps quiet so she won't disturb other people.

She is using good manners.

Charles wants to find a book on dinosaurs. He says "Please" when he asks a librarian for help.

He is using good manners.

Ruth helps her little sister find a sing-along video. They are careful with the videos, books, and computers in the library.

They are using good manners.

Grace loves to learn about lions. Still, she checks out only the number of books she knows she'll read.

She is using good manners.

Mark's books are due on Friday.
He returns his books on time.

He is using good manners.

During story time, Joey and Tonya sit quietly and listen.

They are using good manners.

You can learn a lot at the library. You can also have fun. By using good manners, you can make sure everyone else enjoys his or her visit, too.

About the Author

Carrie Finn never thought she would write books, much less books for children. However, after spending so much time with her 16 nieces and nephews, something must have rubbed off on her.

Carrie has been teaching college writing and literature since 1999 and is a little shocked by the fact that she has had a "first day of school" every fall since 1981. She stays busy by grading papers, baking bread from scratch, talking to the miniature donkeys on the farm near her house, and actively avoiding weeding her garden.

Carrie currently lives in Waterloo, Iowa, with her husband and trusty sidekick, Dan.

About the Illustrator

Chris Lensch attended the Columbus College of Art and Design, and graduated in 1989 with a B.F.A. In 1994, after a move to Colorado, Chris began freelancing full time.

Since then, he has produced work for major corporate clients. His work has also been featured in many national publications. He has received awards from the Society of Illustrators of Los Angeles, How, Graphis, Step-by-Step, American Illustration, the Society of Publication and Design, and Lürzer's Archive.

His illustrations have been published in books by Picture Window Books, Piggy Toes Press, Gamewright, Peaceable Kingdom, and other educational publishers. He now lives in northern Michigan with his wife, three children, a needy labradoodle, and a cranky parakeet.

To Learn More

More to Read

Ashley, Susan. *I Can Use the Telephone*. Milwaukee: Weekly Reader Early Learning Library, 2005.

Candell, Arianna. *Mind Your Manners: In School*. Hauppauge, N.Y.: Barron's, 2005.

DeGezelle, Terri. *Manners at a Restaurant*. Mankato, Minn.: Capstone Press, 2004.

DeGezelle, Terri. *Manners on the Playground*. Mankato, Minn.: Capstone Press, 2005.

Wheeler, Valerie. *Yes, Please! No, Thank You!* New York: Sterling, 2005.

Willems, Mo. *Time to Say Please!* New York: Hyperion, 2005.

On the Web

FactHound offers a safe, fun way to find Web sites related to manners. All of the sites on FactHound have been screened by our staff.

1. Visit www.facthound.com
2. Type in this special code: 1404850937
3. Click on the FETCH IT button.

Your trusty FactHound will fetch the best Web sites for you!

Index